THE LONDON
Ritz
BOOK OF
Customs and Manners

'Manners are of more importance than laws . . . .
Manners are what vex or soothe
corrupt or purify, exalt or debase
barbarize or refine us,
by a constant, steady, uniform, insensible operation
like that of the air we breathe in.'

John Burke (1787–1848)

THE LONDON

Ritz

BOOK OF

Customs and Manners

—————JENNIE REEKIE—————

Ebury Press
LONDON

Published in Great Britain by Ebury Press
an imprint of the Random Century Group
Random Century House
20 Vauxhall Bridge Road
London SW1V 2SA

Text and illustrations copyright
© Random Century Group 1991

**British Library Cataloguing in
Publication Data**
Reekie, Jennie
London Ritz book of customs and manners.
— (Ritz series)
I. Title   II. Series
395
ISBN 0-7126-4860-7

Filmset in Monophoto Goudy by
Advanced Filmsetters (Glasgow) Ltd., Glasgow
Printed in Hong Kong by
L. Rex Printing Co. Ltd.

Acknowledgements
The publishers would like to thank the
following for permission to reprint copyright
material:

Pages 8 and 9 reprinted by permission of
Aurum Press from *The London Ritz: A Social
and Architectural History* by Hugh
Montgomery-Massingberd and David Watkin

Pages 11 and 58 reprinted by permission of
Punch Magazine

Pages 13, 22 and 34 reprinted by permission of
Nigel Nicolson, executor for
Harold Nicolson from *Good Behaviour*,
published by Constable

Page 20 reprinted by permission of Oxford
University Press from *Victorian England—
Portrait of an Age* by G. M. Young

Pages 20, 48 and 57 reprinted by permission of
Hutchinson Ltd (and Peters, Fraser and
Dunlop for Australia and USA) extracts from
P. G. Wodehouse

Page 24 reprinted by permission of Ebury
Press from Jean Shrimpton, *An Autobiography*

Pages 40 and 44 reprinted by permission of
Warner Chappell Music Limited extracts from
Cole Porter

Pages 46 and 54 reprinted by permission of the
Emily Post Institute from *Emily Post's Etiquette*

Page 47 reprinted by permission of Peters,
Fraser and Dunlop from Hilaire Belloc's
Cautionary Tales

Editors: Lansing Andolina, Emma Callery
Illustrator: Rodney Shackell

Contents

Preface

One thing that writers and philosophers have always been agreed upon is that manners are the core of civilization. They govern the way in which people behave and react to each other—be it in a high-tech, twentieth-century home or a remote jungle encampment—and thus are more important and of greater value than ordinary laws. Jonathan Swift explained that 'Those inferior duties of life which the French call *les petites morales* or the smaller morals, are with us distinguished by the name of good manners', and the words 'morals' and 'manners' both come from the Latin *mos*—plural *mores*—meaning manners or customs.

Over the centuries, the view of what constitutes good and bad manners has changed and is, indeed, still changing. One nineteenth-century book on etiquette entitled *Manners and Rules of Good Society* assessed the situation succinctly when discussing table manners: 'It was no rapid revolutionary change in manners that brought about the difference that now exists between the Elizabethan and Victorian eras; no polished Mentor came forward to teach that it was not the nicest and cleanest thing to do to put knives in the salt, to dip fingers into the plates or to spread butter with he thumb; on the contrary, these things righted themselves little by little, step by step, while the present code of manners was arrived at. But it is quite possible that, a hundred years hence, it will be discovered that the manners of 1886 offered wide scope for improvement.'

As we now know, the good lady writer was mistaken, for there have never been as many rules concerning manners and etiquette as existed during the Victorian and Edwardian eras. With hindsight, too, one can see that some of their 'rules of good society' were not only restrictive and unnecessary, but almost unkind. They sometimes lacked the essential aspect of good manners—do unto others as you wish they would unto you—for the sake of propriety.

Today, it would be good to think that those manners and customs which were snobbish and ridiculous have been disposed of, and only those which improve civilization, such as respect for the elderly and consideration of others, retained. For example, the stance The Ritz takes in insisting on gentlemen wearing a tie for afternoon tea may appear old-fashioned and out of date. The reason, as Michael Twomey, the long-time head waiter of the Palm Court explains, is that for many of those sipping their Earl Grey tea and trifling with a cucumber sandwich or frivolous French pastry, it is an *occasion*. One which they may have looked forward to for several weeks, and for which they have dressed up. For them, therefore, it would be offensive if the gentlemen at the next table were casually attired in jeans, trainers and T-shirts. It is no hardship to be properly dressed and it is a classic sign of respect for another's feelings.

The gentle mind by gentle deeds is known
For a man by nothing is so well bewrayed
As by his manners

Edmund Spenser (1552–99)

Royal Ritz

César Ritz, the founder of both the Paris and London Ritz hotels, had a long association with the British Royal Family, going back to 1880 when he was the manager of the Grand Hotel in Monte Carlo. When Queen Victoria was staying at Menton, she and her Highland servant, John Brown, drove over several times to eat there and in 1881 the Prince of Wales reserved a suite of rooms during the summer season.

In 1889, when Ritz took over as manager of the newly-opened Savoy Hotel, it was immediately patronized by the Prince of Wales and other 'members of the British and European Royal families came to dine including the Duc d'Orléans accompanied by his two pet tiger cubs'. Indeed, when César Ritz left the Savoy Hotel after a disagreement with the management, the Prince of Wales promptly cancelled a proposed party with the words, 'Where Ritz goes, I go'.

The Prince of Wales became an enthusiastic supporter of first the Paris Ritz (transferring his allegiance from the Hotel Bristol and then the London Ritz when it opened in 1906. With his death in 1910, the London Ritz lost its most important and prestigious patron. However, his place was soon taken by his grandson and the hotel, as chronicled by

Hugh Montgomery Massingberd and David Watkin in their history of The London Ritz, was 'then at its most fashionable, young and smart. Dancing in the underground ballroom and dining upstairs in probably the most beautiful setting in London was a novel and exciting adventure, frequently given an extra *frisson* by the presence of the embryo prince Charming, the Prince of Wales. Lady Diana Cooper said that some of the stuffier figures in society held out against the new fashion for going to The Ritz—an hotel was, by definition, vulgar—but it was the Prince of Wales who made them change their attitudes.

'Diana Cooper particularly remembers an occasion when the rich American hostess Mrs Gordon was giving a party at The Ritz for her daughter "Baby" (later to marry a French duke). "Several mamas stuck out against Mrs G and would not let their girls go, but when they heard that the young Prince of Wales was going to the party, they gave in..." The party itself was "fabulous". At one stage, "an enormous gilded basket of flowers was brought in; an exquisite female leg appeared—that of Pavlova, who then proceeded to dance".'

After the First World War, the Prince of Wales continued to frequent The Ritz and it is said that it was at The Ritz that Queen Elizabeth the Queen Mother, when Duchess of York, first ordered a meal from a restaurant menu. Between the two wars, in many ways The Ritz was more like an exclusive club than an hotel, for everyone knew everyone. Shortly before his death, Sir Michael Duff said that he looked back 'with great love and nostalgia to those halcyon days of The Ritz before the last war'. It was:

'very much part of my daily life when I was in London in my early days in the 1930s. It had a special atmosphere about it and the Palm Court was always filled before luncheon with "society beauties", debutantes and their boy friends, and famous actors and actresses—though the latter seldom seemed to actually lunch there. Bejewelled American ladies used to parade up and down the corridor awaiting their guests. The Ritz was more like a club than an hotel; you were bound to see your friends there. To "meet at The Ritz" was the obvious choice. It had the combination of elegance and cosiness. The Ritz had an essentially happy atmosphere which radiated from the staff. All the waiters knew everybody and became personal friends. The Ritz in those days had a courtesy and elegance unlike any other hotel; it was thought of as "home" in a sense that never applied to anywhere else.'

The Ritz may no longer have such a club atmosphere, but many of its regular clientele know each other for they include household names from the worlds of showbusiness and finance, as well as members of the aristocracy whose families have been coming to the hotel since it first opened. Members of the Royal Family regularly attend private parties and it is not that rare an occurrence to see one of them enjoying a quiet drink at the bar with a friend or eating in the restaurant.

Royal Commands

* You would never be invited to an event by the Queen and the Queen Mother, rather, you would be commanded to attend and while you would not be sent to the Tower of London for refusing, few excuses are acceptable. A prior engagement is insufficient reason, unless it is a commitment which, if you do not honour, would either cause severe inconvenience to a number of other people or adversely affect your business. If, for example, you have spent six months organizing a meeting with some Japanese regarding an important export order, the Queen would prefer you to meet the Japanese rather than herself! Similarly, rather than accepting the invitation, you would obey the command.

* Invitations from the Queen are always sent out on her behalf by a member of her household, such as the Lord Chamberlain or the Master of the Household and read, 'The Lord Chamberlain (or whoever) is commanded by Her Majesty the Queen to invite . . .' The invitation is never accepted, but the command is obeyed and compliments presented, all in the third person.

* Invitations from other members of the Royal Family are not commands and can be refused if necessary.

$\mathcal{M}$eeting Royalty

* If invited to any event by royalty, be it a lunch party, investiture, garden party or whatever, the Palace has staff who will happily answer any questions you may have prior to the event. You have only to telephone or write to their Private Secretaries. The same applies if you know you are going to be presented to

them at the opening of a new factory, civic function, charity affair or similar event. All the Royal Family are extremely adept at putting people at their ease, whether they are the host(ess) or a guest.

* On being presented to a member of the Royal Family, ladies curtsey—not in the manner of a ballerina, but a little bob with the weight on the right foot which should be in front. Gentlemen bow from the neck. If the Royal hand is extended, the curtesy or bow is executed at the same time.

* The Queen and Queen Mother are addressed as 'Your Majesty' on the first occasion and 'Ma'am' (to rhyme with am, and not arm) on subsequent occasions. Prince Philip and other members of the Royal Family, including their wives but not their husbands, are initially addressed as 'Your Royal Highness' and then 'Sir' or 'Ma'am'. The latter are simply addressed as 'Sir'.

* When speaking to royalty, the terms *you* and *your* are never used but, instead use Your Majesty/Royal Highness, *e.g.* 'If your Majesty would like to', or 'I hope Your Royal Highness had a pleasant flight.' When referring to the Queen or Queen Mother in conversation with other members of royalty or within their hearing you use 'Her Majesty' or 'The Queen' or 'The Queen Mother'. The children of the Sovereign are referred to as 'His/Her Royal Highness, The . . .' and the same applies to Prince Philip, but omit 'The' for other Royals, *e.g.* 'His Royal Highness, Prince Michael of Kent'. If making an introduction, use only the name of the person being introduced, so 'Your Royal Highness, may I present Mr William Jones?'.

In 1969 Basil Boothroyd was commissioned to write the biography of the Duke of Edinburgh and was invited to spend a weekend with the Royal Family during a shooting party at Sandringham to get to know His Royal Highness. He was met at the station by the Queen's Equerry, known to everyone as Jock.

' I leaned on him heavily that weekend. He answered all my nervous questions. Mealtime, tipping who was who in the rest of the party, right up to my closing doubts about the thank-you letter. Prince Philip had invited me. The Queen was my hostess. "Oh, do write to her," said Jock. "She loves getting them." I worried about addressing the envelope. "Just put 'The Queen' and send it to me. I'll see she gets it." It all seemed agreeably casual.

But even he could hardly help with the writing. I scrapped several drafts, including one with something about having been entertained royally.

One of the things I asked him was whether someone could be found to drive me round the estate on the Sunday afternoon. He tied a mental knot in his handerchief, and presently came to my room to say the Land-Rover was at the door, which it was, Prince Philip waiting at the wheel without noticeable impatience. Jock had found someone.

Inside the crowded sitting room at Wood Farm my hostess soon approached, in jeans and an orange jumper and stepping over retrievers. "I'm afraid", were her first words, "we seem to have an enormous lot of dogs in here". What did I say? That that was perfectly all right? '

Punch (June 1987)

'Is there one word which may serve as a rule of practice for all one's life? The master said, Is not reciprocity such a word? What you do not want done to yourself, do not do to others.'

Confucius (551–479 BC)

Writing to Royalty

* If you would like a member of the Royal Family to attend a function, you should first either telephone or write to their Private Secretary to find out if the request and/or date is likely to be favourably received. This should be done at least six months in advance, for their diaries become very booked. If the reply from the Private Secretary is favourable, a letter is sent via the Private Secretary, officially inviting the person concerned. Royalty are never sent a printed invitation.

* When writing to the Queen or the Queen Mother, the opening of the letter reads 'Madam, with my humble duty' and closes with 'I have the honour to be (or 'to remain' if one has written before) your Majesty's humble and obedient servant'. Letters to other members of the Royal Family open 'Dear Sir' or 'Dear Madam' and close in the same way as letters to the Queen, but replacing 'Your Majesty' with 'Your Royal Highness'. Envelopes are addressed to 'Her Majesty the Queen' or 'Queen Mother' or 'His/ Her Royal Highness The Duke of York'.

* Letters of thanks are sent if you have attended an event at the Palace (other than a Garden Party for which it is not essential) or if a member of the Royal Family has been the guest of honour at a function you have organized. In the case of the Queen, letters are sent to the Master of the Royal Households, asking him to convey your thanks to Her Majesty. Letters to other members of the Royal Family are best sent to the appropriate Private Secretary.

Royal Ascot Applications

* Every few years, the list for admission to the Royal Enclosure at Ascot is re-opened and applications can be sent to Her Majesty's Representative at St James's Palace. Notices appear in the court pages of *The Times*, *The Daily Telegraph* and *The Independent* around December and applications are made as early as possible. The letter is written in the third person along the lines of 'Mr and Mrs John Smith present their compliments to Her Majesty's Representative and wish to apply for admission to the Royal Enclosure'. A sponsorship form is then sent, which must be signed by someone who has been admitted to the Royal Enclosure on at least four previous occasions and is prepared to vouch for the good name of the applicant.

Those on the list already apply for vouchers each year, both for themselves and for members of their family. Offspring between the ages of 16 and 25 are entitled to junior vouchers and their ages are stated on each application. Again, the letter is written in the third person, presenting one's compliments to Her Majesty's Representative. Parents who have been admitted apply for their children even at times when the list is closed, although they may be restricted to attendance on certain days to start with.

 Foreign visitors wishing to apply for admission to the Royal Enclosure do so via their embassy.

 If you are issued with a voucher but you are unable to attend, return it to the Royal Ascot Office.

'I am not in the least ashamed of preferring polite people to rude people, cultivated people to uncultivated people or the gifted to the dumb.'

Good Behaviour,
Harold Nicolson (1886–1968)

Debutantes

 When young girls were educated by governesses in the schoolroom until the age of sixteen or seventeen, their social circle was necessarily limited to their relations and immediate neighbours. It was, therefore, important for them to 'come out' and be launched into society. The dual objects of the exercise were first to try to find a husband, and second to widen their circle of female friends.

 The start of the season was in the spring, when the young girls were presented at Court. Queen Victoria used to hold four 'drawing rooms' a year, two before Easter and two after. Any lady who had previously been presented could attend these 'drawing rooms' but convention decreed that you only attended one in any one year. It was also unnecessary to attend a 'drawing room' every year after you had been presented—every other year being more than sufficient, or even once in five years. Once a girl had been presented, she had to be re-presented after her marriage, and then again if her husband succeeded to a title or her first husband died and she re-married.

AT THE PRESENTATION

✱ Presentation was made by a relative or close friend who had previously been presented and while the presentor did not actually accompany the person being presented, she had to be in attendance at the 'drawing room' on that particular day. When planning to introduce a young girl at Court, the lady who was chaperoning always had to write to the Lord Chamberlain informing him of the fact.

✱ Doing the right thing was all important at the presentation. 'A lady on being presented kisses the Queen's hand and should place her hand beneath Her Majesty's who extends it to the lady presented for her to kiss which she should kiss while curtseying. Peeresses and daughters of peers do not kiss the Queen's hand, as Her Majesty kisses them on the cheek or forehead instead.' Debutantes wore long white dresses, 'viz low bodices, short sleeves and train to dress not less than three yards and a half in length.'

✱ There was an equivalent ceremony for gentlemen, know as a levée, when they were presented to the Sovereign or, in the case of Queen Victoria, to her heir or her consort. The main difference was that the presentations were rarely made by a relative, but more usually by the head of a department—such as the Foreign Office or Diplomatic Corps, or by a higher ranking service officer. A gentleman had to be re-presented at every stage of his career.

✱ Presentations at Court ceased in 1958, Queen Elizabeth II considering the practice to be archaic and out-moded.

A True Gentleman

A gentleman is defined as 'A man of gentle birth; one entitled to bear arms, though not noble; A man of chivalrous instinct and fine feelings', and it is these last assets which have always been more highly prized by intelligent members of society than a mere coat of arms. True, in every generation there have been appalling snobs, such as Sir Walter Elliot in Jane Austen's *Persuasion* who held the opinion that a certain curate could not possibly be a gentleman since he was not a man of property! However, breeding does not necessarily make a gentleman, nor is it a title that can simply be conferred on someone, a fact that either James I or Charles II (the following words are ascribed to both!) was well aware of:

The King was asked by a loyal and devoted servant if he could make her son a gentleman, to which he replied that 'he could make a knight or a baronet, but only God Almighty could make a gentleman'. As Daniel Defoe commented, 'The King understood what went to that qualification and that a title no more made a gentleman than the lyon's skyn would make the ass a lyon. The gentleman must have the merit, or he is not at all advan'd by his title; the Sir no more makes a gentleman than the scarf makes a doctor.'

The Victorian writer, G J Whyte Melville considered that: 'Neither birth, nor riches, nor education, nor manner suffice to constitute a gentleman; specimens are to be found at the plough, the loom and the forge, in the rankes and before the mast, as well as in the officers' messroom, the learned professions and the Upper House itself. To our fancy a gentleman is courteous, kindly, brave and high-principled, considerate towards the weak and self-possessed amongst the strong. High-minded and unselfish "He does to others as he would they do unto him".'

Consideration of others

Harold Nicolson thought the foundation of all good manners was 'the development from egoism to consideration for others' and consideration for other people's feelings was what the Reverend Smythe Palmer felt was one of the most important attributes of a gentleman. In 1892, he published a book entitled *The Perfect Gentleman*—a compilation of quotations from a variety of sources on the definition of a gentleman. In the preface to the book he illustrates his point with this delightful true story which took place in India.

'A young soldier in an English regiment had been promoted from the ranks and given a commission in another regiment. According to custom, he was invited to a farewell dinner by the officers of his old regiment and, as the guest of the evening, he was placed on the right of the presiding colonel and helped to all the dishes

first. A fine young fellow, he was, but little used to the ways of the polite world and the *agrémens* of the dining table. The colonel, one of the truest types of gentleman, did his best to put his guest at ease. The soup having been served, a servant came to the guest's side holding a large bowl which contained simply lumps of ice for cooling the champagne. The new-made officer did not know what to make of this bowl. "Ice sir?" asked the servant. The colonel chatted merrily to him on his left. Others of the party began to see his dilemma. "Ice sir?" again asked the waiter. The guest, in ignorant desperation, took up a piece of ice and, not knowing what to do with it, put it in his soup! A smile played lightly on the faces of some of the younger officers. But when the bowl was offered to the colonel, who went on chatting with the guest, without moving a muscle of his face, he also dropped a piece of ice into his soup. Those who came afterwards took their cue from the colonel or let the bowl pass; and the novice breathed freely again to think that, after all, he had done the right thing. That little act of delicate consideration for another's feelings was rightly characterized as an act distinctive of a true gentleman. *)*

'The sone of ane prince, beand [being] distut of vertue, is not ane gentil man, ande in opposit, ane sone of ane mechanyc plebian, beand verteous he is an gentil man.'

The Complaynt of Scotland,
R Henryson (1548)

*L*ittle Courtesies to Ladies

In these days of equality, many of the everyday courtesies extended to ladies which were *de rigeur* until the Second World War have dropped into disuse, but there are still some small gestures which are appreciated.

✱   Victorian and Edwardian gentlemen needed to be possessed of sound knees for they were expected to hop in and out of their chairs not only when a lady entered or left a room but when any lady present stood up. Clearly this was excessive behaviour, but it is still common for a gentleman to stand up the first time a lady walks into the room or takes her leave.

✱   While all but the aged and infirm of the female sex are perfectly capable of opening and shutting a door for themselves, if a gentleman happens to be standing in reasonable proximity, it is chivalrous to open the door for a lady and, if they both arrive at a door at the same moment, to let her pass through first. The car may have replaced the carriage which was not the easiest of vehicles to enter and alight from, especially in long, voluminous dresses. Even so, it is still considered to be good manners to open a car door for a lady and make sure she is happily ensconced.

✱   Traditionally, gentlemen always walk on the outside of the pavement, nearest the street, even if in the company of two ladies. This custom dates back to the days of horse-drawn vehicles as, from this position, a gentleman could more easily protect the lady or ladies from both the horses and carriages which not

Club Behaviour

George Augustus Sala declared that:

> ‘The English are the only clubbable people on the face of the earth. The proper club for the Frenchman is his café, for without women to admire him or to admire, your Monsieur cannot exist. The Russian has more of the clubbable element in him, but the clubs will never flourish in Muscovy till a man can be morally certain that the anecdote he is telling his neighbour will not be carried with notes and emendations in half an hour to the Grand Master of Police. ’

The Gentlemen's Clubs of London remain the last bastion of male society reputed to be peopled by elderly gentlemen reading newspapers who frown when the silence is broken by another member coughing. This is a distinct exaggeration, for the truth is that most clubs are still well patronized by members of all ages at

---

infrequently mounted the pavement. It also helped to preserve the ladies from the muck and refuse which littered the streets as well as presenting a defence to any marauders.

* Ladies have always kept their hats on inside the house, indeed Mrs Beeton specifically advises a lady when paying calls that ‘she may remove her boa or neckerchief; but neither her shawl or bonnet’. Gentlemen, on the other hand, have always removed their hat on entering a house. When meeting a lady of his acquaintance either in the street or at a public gathering, such as a race meeting, it is not necessary for a gentleman to remove his hat but he touches it as a mark of respect.

‘Well it would serve to cure him of an absurd practice of never asking a question at an inn, which he had adopted when quite a young man, on the principle of its being very ungenteel to be curious.

“The notions of a young man of one or two and twenty” said he “as to what is necessary in manners to make him quite the things, are more absurd, I believe, than those of any other set of beings in the world.”’

Persuasion, Jane Austen (1775–1817)

lunchtime. Even so, nothing compares with the club's heyday in the nineteenth and first half of the twentieth centuries when members gathered not only to lunch but also to dine, enjoy a drink in the evening or while away part of the day, as well as to stay.

Many gentlemen considered their club to be their second home. Surtees described a club as where 'A man feels that he has a real substantial home—a home containing every imaginable luxury, without the trouble of management or forethought— a house that goes on as steadily in his absence as during his presence, to which he has not even the trouble of writing a note to say he is coming, to find everything perfectly as he left it.' Indeed, some gentlemen spent more time at their clubs than in their own homes. One despairing nineteenth-century bride bemoaned in her diary 'We have now been married exactly a year in which time my husband has dined with me but once. Every other night he dined at Mr Brook's Club.' Anachronistic as these institutions might appear, it should be remembered that it is the rules of these clubs, some of which like Brooks and Whites were founded in the late seventeenth and early eighteenth centuries, which still govern every other club throughout the world be it a tennis, golf or yacht club or even a bridge club.

✱ It is usual for anyone wishing to join a club to have to be proposed and seconded by members. In most clubs, once a vacancy occurs it is then purely a formality for the person to be elected by the committee. Occasionally, however, someone wishing to become a member is 'blackballed' by an existing member. It is rare

for this situation to arise for, in the unlikely event of the proposer and seconder being informed there is opposition to their candidate, the candidate generally retires rather than subject the proposer and seconder to the embarrassment of his being refused admission. In some clubs, the proposer and seconder would even find it imperative to resign.

The term 'blackballing' derives from the days when if a ballot had to be taken in a club, those entitled to vote put into the ballot box a white ball signifying yes, or agreement with the policy put forward, or no with a black ball. Rules varied. In some clubs, one black ball was sufficient to prevent a man from becoming a member while in others it would be a percentage or straightforward majority.

* Once elected a member, it is important that the rules of a club are read carefully for although most rules are a question of common sense and good manners, some clubs have their own particular rules which everyone, including new members, is expected to know and adhere to. For example, in clubs to which children are admitted with their parents, it can be against club rules for a nanny, au pair or similar paid employee to accompany the family. Some clubs also have a few unwritten rules and the proposer should always run through any of these with the would-be member.

* Many of the Gentlemen's Clubs in London originally did not allow members to bring in guests and it was also frowned upon to buy another member a drink—everyone bought their own. These rules have largely been abolished or have simply died out and, in most clubs, members are allowed to bring in guests although they are sometimes restricted to certain days or times and a limit put on the number one can admit during the course of a week or month.

* As a guest in a friend or acquaintance's club, it is best to remember you are just that—a guest—and behave accordingly. Drinks cannot be ordered by guests from the waiter or the bar nor can they be paid for. If you and your host have made a prior arrangement that you will share the cost of a meal or other expenses, that is a personal matter which should be settled privately and not in full view of other members of the club.

Gentleman's Agreements

* 'My word is my bond' is the basis of a Gentleman's Agreement—a contract founded on honour rather than law. Until very recently, much of the business conducted in the City of London was done entirely on Gentlemen's Agreements and it was rare for a party to renegue on a deal.

Anyone doing so was completely ostracized from society and while that threat may not hold quite the terror it once did, even today few people face the idea of being cut off from their peers with equanimity. A true gentleman always keeps his word.

A Real Lady

Few things have changed more in the last 150 years than society's idea of how a lady should behave. The Victorian species was expected to do little other than supervise her home and servants, perhaps indulge in a little charity work and spend the remainder of her time visiting or attending parties—unless she was in mourning which, sadly, occupied many a month or more, but at least gave her a little respite from the social merry-go-round.

Marriage was the sole aim of every young girl as soon as she had left the schoolroom for it gave her a place in society which a single woman could never hope to aspire to.

Single women, for example, no matter if they were the 50-year-old daughter of a duke, were unable to introduce anyone at court. Unmarried girls were never allowed out without a chaperone—the latter, in some cases, being a married sister scarcely older that the spinster in question but who, because she had a ring on her finger, had status.

Young ladies were expected to merely pick at their food at dinner parties and were effectively barred, on the grounds that it was unladylike, to eat anything considered rich or strong in flavour such as game, or even beef. A lady had to attain middle-age before she was allowed to trifle with such delicacies, which were held to be more suitable fare for gentlemen. Even cheese was strictly taboo.

Harold Nicolson found the idea of such restrictions appalling and in *Good Behaviour* had this comment to make on the life of a Victorian debutante:

> ' Many Victorian young ladies did I suppose struggle to conform to this exacting model. The only one of them I knew personally was my grandmother, who died in 1919 in her hundredth year. There was nothing meek, or unconscious, or dove-like about my grandmother. She was a vigorous and intelligent old lady who bullied her family, bullied her servants, bullied the vicar, bullied the local tradesmen, bullied her neighbours and was universally respected and beloved. I asked her once whether in her youth she had shared and practised these proprieties. She said that she had practised them, that she now thought them idiotic and that at the time they had rendered her gawky, unhappy and actually ill. She told me that her contemporaries had been told that Brummell had broken off his engagement when he discovered that his fiancée liked cabbage and that Byron had mentioned that it made him sick to see a woman eat. The early nineteenth century maidens would thus starve themselves in public and then get their maids to bring wads of cake and ham and chicken to their bedrooms. "It was all most unpleasant" said my grandmother. "I much wish that I had been young at some other period of history." '

It was not until the end of the nineteenth century that it started to become socially acceptable for ladies to dine in public places such as restaurants and hotels. Lily Langtry was one of the first to break with tradition when she began dining at the Savoy (where César Ritz was the manager) in the 1890s with the Prince of Wales (Edward VII). Previously, Ritz had managed the Grand Hotel Nationale in Lucerne where, as his widow later recorded,

> ' as early as the eighties, great ladies such as the Duchesse de Rochefoucauld, the Duchesse de Maille, the Contesse de Greffulhe, Lady Leache, Lady Greville, the Duchess of Leeds and the Duchess of Devonshire, appeared in the public ballrooms and dining room and lent their enthusiastic support to the special fêtes there which Ritz organized. In Paris or London at that time, they would have preferred to be found dead than to be caught in a public hotel dining room. '

Today, ladies face totally different challenges to those of their Victorian counterparts, but the one thing they have in common is manners, for they are the distinguishing mark of a lady, no matter what social class she may come from or aspire to. In 1380, William of Wykeham, when he founded Winchester School gave it as its motto the immortal words 'Manners Makyth Man'—the only alteration to be made to that today would be 'and Woman'

$\mathcal{V}$isiting

The paying and receiving of calls occupied a considerable part of each day for ladies during the nineteenth and early part of the twentieth centuries. Countless rules governed calling which, if not obeyed to the letter, were likely to render the offender a social outcast as the aristocratic (and autocratic) writer of *Manners and Rules of Good Society* was at pains to point out.

' Ladies stand upon strict and ceremonious etiquette with each other regards both paying and receiving calls. Ignorance or neglect of the rules which regulate paying calls, bring many inconveniences in its train; for instance when a lady neglects to pay a call due to an acquaintance, she runs the risk of herself and her daughters being excluded from entertainments given by the said acquaintance. '

It was, for example, considered very bad form not to call on someone within a week if you had dined at their home or attended a ball or picnic; there was very strict protocol on who could call on whom, depending on their place in society and the returning of calls made by others. Mrs Beeton divided calls 'under three heads, those of ceremony, friendship and congratulation or condolence' and the latter should

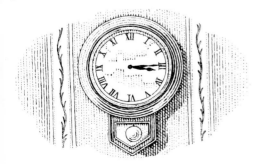

be paid 'within a week after the event which occasions them. If the acquaintance, however, is slight, then immediately after the family have appeared at public worship. A lady should send her card, and if her friends be able to receive her, the visitor's manner and conversation should be subdued and in harmony with the character of her visit.'

While always referred to as 'morning' calls, these visits were actually made in the afternoon. 'Morning', in this case, meaning that they took place prior to dinner in the evening, rather than before noon. The only people whom one could visit before luncheon were *very* intimate friends and family when a lady could sit in her 'darned cap and collar'. The time for 'morning calls' was between 3 and 6 pm. The first hour was the 'ceremonious hour', the second was 'semi-ceremonious', and the final hour was 'without ceremony and wholly for friends'.

Fifteen minutes was the duration of a ceremonious call—a timing it could be difficult to ascertain if the drawing room did not boast a conspicuous clock. In Mrs Gaskell's *Cranford*, the question was reasonably asked 'How am I to find out when a quarter of an hour has passed?' to which the reply was 'You must keep thinking about the time, my dear and not allow yourself to forget it in conversation.'

Conversation was all-important, and it was the duty of the hostess not to allow it to flag. Under no circumstances was she allowed to produce 'albums of photographs, books, illustrated newspapers, portfolio drawings, and artistic efforts of members of the family' in order to help pass the time; she had to be totally self-reliant on her powers of small talk to entertain the guests. Mrs Beeton also points out that 'the occupations of drawing, music or reading should be suspended on the entrance of morning visitors. If a lady, however, be engaged with light needlework, and none other is appropriate in the drawing room, it may not be, under some circumstances, inconsistent with good breeding, to quietly continue it during conversation.'

With ceremonious calls occupying such a comparatively short space of time, it was possible to make several visits in one afternoon, ending up with a less formal, and slightly longer, call on a friend. Everyone had certain days when they called and at least one when they were always At Home—a fact they either conveyed personally to those they visited, saying 'I am At Home on Thursdays' or whichever day, or wrote upon their visiting cards so that the recipients would know when they might repay the call. At other times, it was more a question of luck as to whether one was found 'at home' or not.

The etiquette surrounding the leaving of visiting cards if all the members of the household were out was equally as complex as that surrounding visiting itself. On being informed that there was no one 'at home' a lady would not only leave her own personal visiting card for the lady of the house, but also two of her husband's—one for the lady of the house and one for *her* husband. In some cases, the right hand corner of the card might be turned down and this either signified that the lady had made the visit personally (as against sending a servant) and/or that the visit had been intended both for the lady of the house and her daughters.

It was also quite common practice for servants to inform visitors that the lady of the house was 'not at home', either meaning that they were not receiving visitors, possibly due to illness, or that they simply did not wish to see those particular acquaintances, something which Mrs Beeton advises against taking offence at.

' The form of words "not at home" may be understood in different senses; but the only courteous way is to receive them as being perfectly true. You may imagine that the lady of the house is really at home, and that she would make an exception in your favour, or you may think that your acquaintance is not desired; but, in either case, not the slightest word is to escape you, which would suggest, on your part, such an impression. '

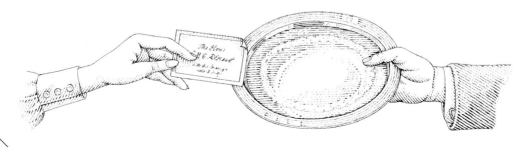

ress

Since the 'Swinging Sixties', codes of dress have relaxed dramatically and other than at formal, or certain sporting occasions, a lady can wear what she feels she looks good in and/or is most comfortable in. Occasionally, this more casual stance can lead to problems in knowing exactly what to wear, and certainly one advantage of the more rigid code of previous years was that there was never any doubt as to what was right and what was wrong. Commonsense is the most important dictum for the majority of events, but there remain a few occasions for which there has traditionally been a correct way to dress.

In 1965, the model Jean Shrimpton went to Australia for the Melbourne Cup, Australia's most prestigious horse-racing event which was sponsored by Orlon. Her role was to wear clothes made from Orlon and to present the prizes after the race, but her choice of outfit caused a tremendous furore as she describes in her autobiography.

' The day of the races was a hot one, so I didn't bother to wear any stockings. My legs were still brown from summer, and as the dress was short it was hardly formal. I had no hat or gloves with me, for the very good reason that I owned neither. I went downstairs cheerfully from my hotel room, regardless of what was to come.

The organizers were waiting in the hall.

"Where is your hat? Where are your gloves?" one of the women asked, looking pointedly at my bare legs.

"Haven't got any," I said. No one moved. I couldn't think why everyone looked so cross.

"Isn't it time to go?" I asked as they hovered, staring at me.

In the limo the promoters had hired to take me to the racecourse I thought the men from the fibre company who were escorting me continued to look cross. Terry [Stamp], smart in his needlecord suit, didn't say anything. He was used to the way I dressed. But when we arrived at the racecourse it didn't take me long to realize I had committed the most terrible faux pas. The Melbourne women, in stockings, hats and long white gloves, were pointing at me and glaring. The men, as usual, didn't take too much notice.

What I had not appreciated was that the Melbourne Cup was the smartest event of the Australian year. The conservative Melbourne matrons in their somewhat out-of-date best were terribly shocked: my appearance was described as insulting and disgraceful. Opinion was that I had been rude and not bothered about an occasion that was important to my hosts and to Australian society generally. They were affronted.

I suppose it was discourteous of me, but any rudeness was unintended. I discovered too late that the sponsors expected me to go all dolled up with hat and gloves, looking like a fashion plate. I was under the delusion that they had hired Jean Shrimpton, the girl next door, the gawky waif— not a clothes horse! '

Jean Shrimpton (1990)

'It is not good manners to show your learning before ladies.'

English Proverb

THE OPERA

Although black tie is by no means essential for gentlemen at the Royal Opera House on an ordinary evening, many choose to wear it and ladies tend to wear smart, cocktail-type dresses. At gala evenings, gentlemen wear white tie and ladies long evening gowns. At Glyndebourne, which is a private house and not a public building, gentlemen are requested to wear black tie and ladies evening dresses. If picnicking outside during the interval, a coat or wrap can be invaluable for it can suddenly become very chilly. The area of the garden eaten in should always be left in immaculate condition—this is only polite.

RACING

In order to gain admission to the Royal Enclosure at Ascot, gentlemen wear morning suits or service or national dress, and ladies very formal daydresses and hats which cover the crown of the head. This code is generally followed by those in the private boxes and by some (but by no means all) in Tattersalls. The same applies in the Members' Enclosure at Epsom on Derby Day, although the clothes worn by the ladies are not quite as smart as those worn at Royal Ascot.

Such formal clothes are not worn to other race meetings, although ladies still frequently wear hats for all the Classic meetings, as well as

on some of the more special days at Ascot, Chester, Goodwood, Newmarket and Sandown. At Goodwood, gentlemen traditionally wear suits and panama hats.

Following Gold Cup day in 1909, *The Times* reported that

'Such fragile material as muslin, laces, nets and soft silks were the only wear. Yesterday it was undeniable that white—including dead white, ivory and ficelle—predominated in the dresses, while black achieved extraordinary success in millinery. A delicate subtle mauve appeared in equally delicate materials. Fine net or ninons, embroidered in filoselle very handsomely worked in bold raised patterns and long coats were among the successes of the day.

Eccentricities to be noticed in some of the fantastic tunics and in one dress of willow-patterned blue and white silk with a wide sash of Chinese blue girdling the waist and hips and tied in a bow at the back, but in front giving a corselet effect. Hats were trimmed with feathers, ospreys, flowers or merely a bow of lace, white, black or metal...'

The Cheltenham Festival is the smartest of the National Hunt meetings, where gentlemen sport smart tweed or plain lounge suits and winter suits are traditional for the ladies. At other meetings, more casual country clothes are worn and very casual country wear is the order of the day at point-to-points.

HENLEY ROYAL REGATTA

This is the one event of the summer season when some of the men outshine the ladies in their dress, for those entitled to wear their school, university or club rowing colours do so with enthusiasm. The sight of a slightly rotund 60-year-old gentleman in a striped blazer, matching cap and garish socks might be a little bizarre but it is the one occasion in the year when he can wear them! The smartest is the pink blazer and socks of the Leander Club for it implies that the wearer either won a cup at Henley, was in a blue boat (rowed for either Oxford or Cambridge in the Boat Race) or rowed for England.

By order of the Stewards, ladies are not permitted to enter the Stewards' Enclosure wearing any form of trousers (and that includes culottes or divided skirts). A hat is not obligatory, but is requested. Gentlemen, if not sporting rowing colours, wear a jacket and tie.

ROYAL GARDEN PARTIES

More usually, morning suits or national dress are worn by gentlemen and ladies wear daydresses with hats, or national dress if they come from abroad.

WIMBLEDON

There is no specific dress for the Lawn Tennis Championships at Wimbledon, but if invited

'Then there is Mrs—oh, I can never remember her name; she lives in a street that the cabmen have never heard of, and is at home on Wednesdays. She frightened me horribly once at a private view by saying mysteriously "I oughtn't to be here, you know; this is one of my days". I thought she meant that she was subject to periodical outbreaks and was expecting an attack at any moment. So embarrassing if she had suddenly taken it into her head that she was Cesare Borgia or St Elizabeth of Hungary. That sort of thing would make one unpleasantly conspicuous even at a private view. However, she merely meant to say that it was Wednesday, which at the moment was incontrovertible.'

Saki (1870–1916)

by a member, gentlemen tend to wear lounge suits and ladies reasonably smart daydresses or their equivalent.

DANCES AND BALLS

At a 'black tie' affair either short or long evening dresses are worn, according to the fashion of the time. For 'white tie', glamorous voluminous and extravagant long dresses are more usual.

BANQUETS

For 'white tie' dinners long evening dresses are appropriate.

The Perfect Hostess

'The art of receiving guests is a very subtle one, difficult to acquire; but when acquired and thoroughly mastered it confers upon a mistress of a house an enviable reputation—that of being a perfect hostess', wrote the author of *Manners and Rules of Good Society* in the last century.

There is no doubt that some ladies find the art of hostessing more difficult to master than others. However, it is quite possible for anyone to perfect the important techniques of making guests feel truly welcome, comfortable and at ease—whether they have come for a quick drink, a dinner party, a dance or the weekend and this can be more readily conveyed by manner and actions than by speech. Time may be of the essence, but little gestures, such as putting flowers in a guest's bedroom or having the ice ready in the ice bucket before they arrive for a drink will make them feel their company is desired and not an inconvenience.

Lavishness is not the secret of the perfect hostess. Those who liberally dispense caviar and champagne often provide poorer entertainment than those who have smaller purses but who are genuinely interested in their guests and go to infinite trouble to gather together the right mixture of people, for this

> *When friends are at your hearthside met,*
> *Sweet courtesy has done it most*
> *If you have made each guest forget*
> *That he himself is hot the host.*
>
> 'Hospitality', T B Aldrich (1836–1907)

is of supreme importance. The hostess who carefully plans her parties and cares about whether her guests will enjoy each other's company is virtually assured of success. For her it will not be a crisis if the soup burns, the soufflé collapses or the dog eats all the canapés for the ambiance she has created will carry her through such minor mishaps. The food and drink that is served at a party is important but it is not all-important—the people are.

Invitations

✳ Invitations to dinner parties are generally issued over the telephone these days which is a great advantage to the hostess for she then knows immediately whether or not her guests are able to accept and if she is trying to get a particular group of people together, to juggle the date so that everyone can attend. 'At Home' cards (a relic from the days when ladies called on each other in the afternoons) can then be sent as a reminder.

✳ 'At Home' cards remain the prerogative of women and if a man's name appears on the invitation then the wording is always 'requests the pleasure of your company'. Helpful host-

esses give their guests some indication as to dress by including 'Informal' or 'Black Tie' on the invitation.

✳ Some hostesses have cards engraved with their names and addresses which are used for different occasions such as drinks parties or buffet suppers. For special occasions, cards can be engraved specifically.

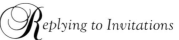

Replying to Invitations

✳ Invitations need to be replied to quickly so that a hostess knows how many she has to cater for. If you are unable to attend, she will want to be made aware of this as early as possible for she may wish to invite someone else. Once an invitation has been accepted, it is extremely bad manners not to attend, unless prevented by illness, bereavement or *very* important business commitments.

✳ Replies are usually written in the third person, *e.g.* 'Mr and Mrs John Smith thank Mrs James Jones for her kind invitation to cocktails at The Ritz on Monday 12th October and have much pleasure in accepting' or 'very much regret they are unable to attend due to a previous engagement, will be abroad' etc. The reply has the address and is dated in the usual way, but it is not signed.

✳ If the invitation is from a close friend, the reply can be in the first person or, if you are unable to attend, a formal reply can be accompanied by a note saying how sorry you are not to be able to accept.

Introductions

* One of the obvious duties of a hostess is to introduce her guests to one another. At a large gathering it is clearly impossible to introduce everyone but an effort should be made to introduce as many people as possible and to regularly look round to check that no one is left on their own or a married couple are not by themselves talking to each other. Equally, a hostess should be wary of being over-solicitous—interrupting an animated conversation between people whom she had introduced only 15 minutes previously is likely to be a somewhat unpopular move.

* At smaller parties and dinner parties, everyone can easily be introduced to each other. Making introductions when both parties are friends is never a problem, but it can be a more daunting task if they are only brief acquaintances, are of a different generation or are some kind of celebrity.

* Pronounce everyone's name as clearly as possible, so that you are not asked to repeat it by one of the parties and always introduce the junior person to the more senior. So, when introducing two people of the same sex, the younger should be introduced to the older, *i.e.* 'Captain White, I would like you to meet Colonel Black' or 'Julia Smith ... Mrs Jones.' The gentleman is always introduced to the lady, *i.e.* Mr Bloggs or Fred Bloggs ... Mrs Smith or Julia Smith. If the gentleman is considerably older and more important, however, it should be the other way round, *i.e.* Julia Smith ... Lord Byron.

FORMS OF ADDRESS FOR THE PEERAGE

While few members of the peerage are likely to be upset if they are addressed incorrectly, the perso
making the error is apt to be mortified so these are the correct forms of social address.

	Introduced as	Addressed as	Envelope	Opening of Letter
Duke	The Duke of London	Duke	The Duke of London	Dear Duke of London or Dear Duke
Duchess	The Duchess of London	Duchess	The Duchess of London	Dear Duchess of London or Dear Duchess
Marquess (*the eldest son of a duke*)	Lord Glasgow	Lord Glasgow	The Marquess of Glasgow	Dear Lord Glasgow
Marchioness	Lady Glasgow	Lady Glasgow	The Marchioness of Glasgow	Dear Lady Glasgow
Younger son of a Duke or Marquess	Lord James Aberdeen	Lord James	Lord James Aberdeen	Dear Lord James
Wife of younger son of a Duke or Marquess	Lady James Aberdeen	Lady James	Lady James Aberdeen	Dear Lady James
Daughter of a Duke, Marquess or Earl	Lady Mary Aberdeen	Lady Mary	Lady Mary Aberdeen	Dear Lady Mary
Earl[1]	Lord Cardiff	Lord Cardiff	The Earl of Cardiff	Dear Lord Cardiff
Countess	Lady Cardiff	Lady Cardiff	The Countess of Cardiff	Dear Lady Cardiff
Viscount (*the eldest son of an Earl*)	Lord Belfast	Lord Belfast	The Viscount Belfast	Dear Lord Belfast
Viscountess[2]	Lady Belfast	Lady Belfast	The Viscountess of Belfast	Dear Lady Belfast

	Introduced as	Addressed as	Envelope	Opening of Letter
Younger son of an Earl or Viscount and sons of Barons	Mr Brighton	Mr Brighton	The Hon Charles Brighton	Dear Mr Brighton
Wife of the above	Mrs Brighton	Mrs Brighton	The Hon Mrs Charles Brighton	Dear Mrs Brighton
Daughters of Viscounts or Barons	Miss Brighton	Miss Brighton	The Hon Emma Brighton	Dear Miss Brighton
Baron	Lord Norwich	Lord Norwich	The Lord Norwich	Dear Lord Norwich
Baron's wife	Lady Norwich	Lady Norwich	The Lady Norwich	Dear Lady Norwich
Baronet	Sir Richard York	Sir Richard	Sir Richard York Bt.	Dear Sir Richard
Wife of Baronet or Knight	Lady York	Lady York	Lady York	Lady York
Knight	Sir Mark Chichester	Sir Mark	Sir Mark Chichester	Dear Sir Mark

Earls can be the eldest sons of Marquesses or they may have an earldom.
Widows of peers are addressed in the same way verbally as before but envelopes are written either to The Dowager Viscountess of Belfast or Jane, Viscountess of Belfast and the latter form of address is also used for divorcées.

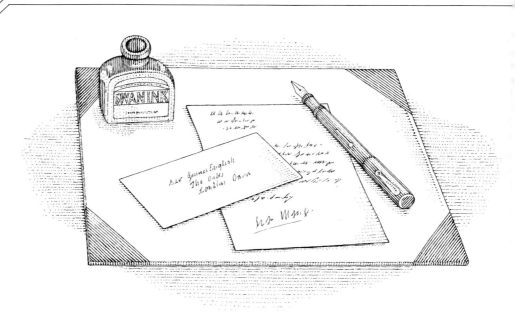

* Since the Second World War, the use of christian names has increased dramatically although the trend first started at the turn of the century, as Harold Nicolson, born in 1886, observed:

'In my own lifetime . . . the feeling about Christian names has changed completely. My father would never have used the Christian name of any man or woman who was not a relation or whom he had not known for at least thirty years. My aunt called her husband by his surname until the day of his death. It was in the reign of Edward VII that the use of Christian names first became fashionable, and even then it was surrounded by all manner of precaution and restrictions. '

The practice of calling people by their christian names has, in many ways, made the art of introduction easier but it has its own pitfalls. For example, if a hostess introduces someone to you as Jamie English how are you to know whether he is Mr English, Dr English, Sir James English or Lord English? It may well be immaterial but if, within five minutes of meeting him, you are called upon to introduce him to someone else and, not wishing to presume on such a brief acquaintance, introduce him as Mr English when he is, in fact, Lord English, it could be embarrassing. Most titled people in that situation will be quite unperturbed and put everyone at their ease by not correcting the introducer or by saying 'Jamie English' or

'Please call me Jamie' but there are others who are a little touchy about their titles. If a hostess is in any doubt at all, even if she is on first name terms with the gentleman, she should introduce him as Lord English or whatever his (or indeed her) title may be. She should also call the other Mrs or Mr unless the person the peer is being introduced to is considerably younger.

✳ When introducing two complete strangers it is helpful to both if you can give them a little hint about each other to facilitate conversation, *e.g.* 'Julia Smith I would like you to meet Mary Jones. Mary, Julia has just returned from Australia and I believe you and your husband were there last year.'

Equally, if there is something important like a political affiliation which it is best for someone to be aware of so that they do not immediately become involved in a heated argument, this point should be made in the introduction, *e.g.* 'Mr Smith...Colonel Black. Mr Smith is the prospective Liberal candidate for this constituency, Colonel.'

✳ If a guest has recently suffered a bereavement or other catastrophe, a hostess should discreetly advise as many of the other guests as possible so that they do not accidently make remarks which could be distressing.

> 'True politeness consists of being easy one's self, and in making everyone about one as easy as one can.'
>
> *Table Talk*, Alexander Pope (1688–1744)

Seating Plans

✳ At dinner and luncheon parties it remains customary for the gentleman considered to be the most important, senior in age or of only slight acquaintance to be placed on the right hand of the hostess and the next senior on her left. Their wives, or ladies of similar position are, in the same way, seated on the host's right and left. However, in these days of equality, few people are likely to take offence if, for some reason, they are placed elsewhere and sociability is increasingly deemed more important than rank. At a very formal meal or banquet, though, care should be taken to seat everyone according to precedence. On these occasions, it is usually self-evident who should sit where and there are exact rules of precedence which can be obtained from *Burke's Peerage*.

✳ While it is obviously easier to seat people if there are an equal number of both sexes, it is no longer thought to be a pre-requisite of a dinner party. At one time, a hostess would pair off a couple and 'send them down' to dinner together. The gentleman would take the lady's arm, escort her from the drawing room to the dining room and then place her on his right hand. An odd number was, consequently, of great inconvenience.

✳ If possible, the sexes should alternate at the table but if two people of the same sex have to sit together it may be best if one of them is the host or hostess—it should certainly not be the person who has come without a partner. The one uneven number you should be careful to avoid is thirteen (the number present at The

Last Supper). Many people consider this to be extremely unlucky and will refuse to sit at the table, fearing it signifies an imminent death.

* Even for informal parties, if there are more than six present, it is a good idea to note down a seating plan on a piece of paper prior to the meal. If the seating is done on the spur of the moment, you may find you have inadvertently put a husband and wife next to each other or two people who are unlikely to get on well together. When planning who should sit next to who, thought should be given to the guests' character and interests. For instance, a shy person should, if possible, be sat beside someone who is naturally gregarious but will not dominate and will try to draw him (or her) out. Equally, all the quiet people should not be put at one end of the table and all the noisy ones at the other, for the noisier element will then take over the table completely. If it is a large dinner party, it may be easier if place names are put on the table so guests may find their place easily.

The question of precedence was one that severely exercised the mind of every nineteenth-century hostess. A copy of *Burke's Peerage* was almost as essential as the dining table itself, if the characters in Jane Austen's novels are anything to go by. Mary Musgrove in *Persuasion*, being the daughter of a baronet, took precedence over her mother-in-law, despite the latter's seniority and it was clearly a subject very close to Mary's heart:

'It was Mary's complaint, that Mrs Musgrove was very apt not to give her the precedence that was due, when they dined at the Great House with other families; and she did not see any reason why she was to be considered so much at home as to lose her place. And one day, when Anne was walking with only the Miss Musgroves one of them, after talking of rank, people of rank and jealousy of rank said "I have no scruples of observing to *you*, how nonsensical some persons are about their place, because all the world knows how easy and indifferent you are about it, but I wish any body could give Mary a hint that it would be a great deal better if she were not so very tenacious; especially, if she would not always be putting herself forward to take place of mamma. Nobody doubts her right to have precedence of mamma, but it would be more becoming in her not to be always insisting on it".'

The Ideal Guest

Being a guest is a good deal less onerous than being a hostess, but it does not absolve one from making an effort to ensure the success of a party, for it is the duty of every guest to try to enjoy themselves, be the occasion a dance, a cocktail party, a dinner party or a house party. The ideal guest is the one who puts himself out to be agreeable to everybody; who is prepared to sit down and talk animatedly to an elderly relative; who is aware of a shy person or stranger in the room and draws them into the general conversation and notices when their host or hostess needs a little assistance. These are the people whose diaries are full, as against the guest who arrives bearing extravagant gifts and then proceeds to be a tedious and insensitive bore.

Few things are more annoying to a hostess than the guest who apparently feels his (or her) *presence* is all that is required of him. The behaviour of the guest who is not pleasant to the other guests, or does not mix with them; who does not join in the entertainments offered which his hostess has gone to lengths to organize, and declines her food is boorish, if not downright rude.

Ideal guests not only enjoy themselves but they do not arrive too late or too early, nor do they outstay their welcome. They eat everything that is put in front of them with alacrity and do not complain that they are on a diet or never eat brussels sprouts. They also answer invitations promptly and, having once accepted, would not dream of letting their hostess down by not turning up, and finally write to or telephone their hostess shortly after the event to thank her.

Dinner Guests

* 'Punctuality is the politeness of kings', said Louis XVIII of France. It is also 'the duty of gentlemen and the necessity of men of business' wrote one Samuel Smith but he might also have added 'and dinner guests' for dinner is a meal for which one should not be late.

* With modern traffic conditions, it is becoming more and more difficult to know exactly how long a journey will take and it is as bad

form to be early for a dinner party as it is to be late. Should you accidently find you are early, you should discreetly wait a little distance from the host or hostess's home and wait until the appointed hour. The same applies if you have been invited as somebody's guest to a restaurant or hotel. If you should arrive a little late and it is obvious that your hostess, although politely offering a drink, really wishes to start dinner immediately, it is good manners to decline.

* Nowadays, conversation is often very general around the table which makes for a more entertaining meal than the Victorian system which, in effect, made dinner parties a series of *têtes à têtes* for then one only had to converse with the lady or gentleman with whom one had been 'sent down' to dinner. According to one manual on etiquette of the period, one could 'if one desired' speak to the other neighbour, but it was not felt to be essential. Small wonder that both sexes were frequently relieved at the arrival of the port so that they could escape their partner's company!

Obviously, even today, if it is a large dinner party seated around a large table, it is all but impossible to speak to anyone other than your immediate neighbours, but conversation should be made naturally between the two of them.

* The practice of leaving the gentlemen with the port at the end of the meal is one that has almost died out. If it should be suggested, though, at least it is now customary for ladies to be offered as fine a quality of port in the drawing room as the gentlemen have in the dining room, and for the host to keep the gentlemen for no longer than 20 minutes.

In Mrs Beeton's day drinks do not appear to have been served prior to dinner. She remarked that the half hour spent before the meal while everyone assembled was one of the most trying for a hostess as she valiantly attempted to entertain her guests, at the same time wondering whether her cook and the rest of the staff would come up to scratch and quotes this little poem:

How sad it is to sit and pine,
The long half hour before we dine!
Upon our watches oft to look,
Then wonder at the clock and cook . . .

And strive to laugh in spite of Fate!
But laughter forced soon quits the room,
And leaves it in its former gloom.
But lo! the dinner now appears
The object of our hopes and fears,
The end of all our pain!

✳ Time of departure will depend very much on the formality of the party—and the success of it. An interval of 30 minutes after the coffee has been served is about the shortest length of time unless you have informed the hostess before dinner that you will have to depart promptly. Equally, if a party is held on a weekday and you are aware that your host and hostess have to work in the morning, or have young children who will be up early, it is inconsiderate to stay late.

ouse Guests

The Roman scholar Plautus is reputedly the first man to have coined the phrase that 'Fish and guests smell in three days'. Certainly, unless a house guest is a very close friend or exceptionally commodious, there are few who are a real pleasure to entertain after this period.

✳ Very often, guests are invited for a weekend to attend an event, such as a point-to-point,

a shoot or concert, in which case the hostess will have planned the weekend around it. The ideal house guest, though, is the one who fits happily into the household and falls in with any plans that are made—no matter what they are—and is just as happy going for a bracing five-mile walk as sitting reading a book by the fire, or round the edge of a swimming pool.

> 'A gentleman never eats. He breakfasts, he lunches, he dines—but he never eats.'
>
> Cole Porter (1893–1964)

✱ Some households still keep a large staff, in which case offers of assistance need not be given, but they are the exception. Offers to help prepare meals, lay tables and wash up usually go down extremely well. But few things are more irritating for a hostess than the guest who wanders into the kitchen, airily enquires if there is anything to be done and, just when a request is about to be made of them, walks out again. The best kind of guests are the ones who notice little tasks that need doing, such as preparing vegetables or clearing away the coffee things and unobtrusively perform them, without asking.

✱ If staying in a household where there are staff (even if they are, to your knowledge, only temporary) it is quite usual for a valet (or possibly the butler) to unpack the gentlemen's suitcases and one of the maids the ladies'. They also re-pack them before departure. These days, the rarity of butlers has made them a rather daunting servant to encounter and while some may appear aloof—and few approve of familiarity—they are generally quite approachable. The main function of the butler is to ensure that the household runs smoothly, be he serving the drinks or attending in the dining room and, to that end, he is responsible for all the other servants.

* Should you suffer an allergy or be a vegetarian, it is best to inform your hostess of this *before* you arrive. Likewise many people are allergic to dogs and cats, and it is preferable for a hostess to know this rather than allow the cat to sit on them and then have a guest suffering a chronic asthma attack.

* No guest should ever take his (or her) own animals to another's house unless it has been agreed upon beforehand. The fact that the 'Jones's have dogs and love animals' is not a good enough reason for you to take your dogs without prior permission—their dogs may be very resentful of strangers and spend the entire weekend attacking yours which will only make for a fraught visit. *No* dog should be taken unless it is thoroughly house-trained and well-mannered and a guest's dog must obey the rules of the house, *i.e.* he may be allowed to sit on the chairs at home but if the house-dogs are not allowed up on the chairs, nor must he be and if he cannot be kept off them should be left at home. Many a weekend has been ruined for

both guests and hosts by the appalling behaviour of one party's animals!

Hotel Guests

* Few things are more irritating to other hotel guests who wish to sit down and engage in quiet conversation, than a noisy group of people who attempt to completely take over the lounge, bar or other public place or who are rude to staff. Good manners means being polite to everyone, be they complete strangers who happen to be staying in the same hotel, or hotel staff. As George Bernard Shaw said, 'The great secret is not having bad manners or good manners or any other particular sort of manners, but having the same manners for all human souls.'

There are usually other guests either side and above and below a hotel bedroom. Music should not be played too loudly nor riotous parties held until the small hours of the morning.

* The staff may be paid to clean and tidy the room but even so guests should make an effort

---

'My idea of good company, Mr Elliott, is the company of clever, well-informed people, who have a great deal of conversation; that is what I call good company.'
'You are mistaken', he said gently, 'that is not good company, that is the best.'

Persuasion, Jane Austin (1775–1817)

to keep their rooms reasonably tidy, so that the chambermaid is not left bemused as to where to start in clearing up the mess.

✱ Any complaints are best made direct to the management, rather than delivering a tirade to a junior member of staff whose fault it may—or may not—be.

Tipping

✱ A dinner guest does not tip staff in private houses but a house guest should tip any resident member of staff who has in any way been of service to them, such as the butler, the cook, or the maid; the chauffeur if he has driven you, or the housekeeper. If you are unsure how much to leave, ask your hostess to advise you for she will not want her guests to appear parsimonious to her staff, nor will she want them to set a precedent by being over-generous. In the case of daily help, check first with your hostess—some people are delighted for them to be tipped, others consider it unnecessary.

✱ At a shoot, the gamekeeper should always be tipped and his tip will vary according to how good the sport has been—a gamekeeper's tip, however, should always err on the generous side. If a loader is employed, he should also be tipped at the end of the day(s), but his tip will be the same, irrespective of the quality of the sport. If in doubt about how much either

should be, ask your host or another gun who shoots regularly. Gillies should also be tipped after a day's fishing. Grooms at riding stables who have turned a horse out well deserve a small tip, as do the lads who 'lead up' horses at the races, even if you only own an ear!

* If a service charge has not been added at a hotel, the chambermaid and head waiter should be tipped at the end of the stay (the latter can then divide the tip between the restaurant staff). Other staff should be tipped at the time they perform the service, such as hall porters if they organize train, airline or theatre tickets, doormen when they call and see you into a taxi (if called upon to check that your car is not being given a parking ticket or being towed away, the tip should be a substantial one), luggage porters and valets.

Presents

* A departing present to a hostess is always a kind gesture. It should be borne in mind, though, that an over-generous present can be an embarrassment to a hostess and an inexpensive one, chosen with care to reflect her interests, may give greater pleasure.

* The present is usually given to the hostess either on arrival or departure, but it can be sent later. A bunch of flowers which arrive the day after guests have left, when the hostess may be feeling a little flat, will lift her spirits instantly; or if she expresses an interest in a book and you then send her a copy, she will deem it a great compliment.

* Giving dinner party hostesses presents is a modern trend and, the more formal the meal, the less it is expected. If wishing to give your host or hostess a small gift, remember that she is unlikely to have time to arrange a bouquet of flowers—a few freesias, on the other hand, take only seconds—and that the wine for the evening will doubtless have been selected, so if you produce a bottle do not be offended if it is put away for another day.

If spitting chance to moove thee so
Thou canst it not forbeare,
Remember do it modestly,
Consider who is there.
If filthiness or ordure thou
Upon the floore doe cast,
Tread out and cleanse it with thye foot,
Let that be done with haste.

Book of Demeanour, Richard Weste (1619)

*B*read and Butter Letters

Thank you so much Mrs Lousborough-Goodby,
  thank you so much,
Thank you for that infinite weekend with you . . .
For the clinging perfume in that damp little room,
For those cocktails so hot, and the bath that was
  not,
For those guests so amusing and mentally bracing,
Who talked about racing and racing and racing.
For the promaine I got from your famous tinned
  salmon,
And the fortune I lost when you taught me
  backgammom,
For those mornings I spent with your dear but deaf
  mother,
For those evenings I passed with that bounder your
  brother,
And for making me swear to myself there and then
Never to go for a weekend again.

Cole Porter (1893–1964)

No matter how much you might like to write a letter of thanks in this vein, don't! Letters of thanks should at least sound sincere and enthusiastic—whether the occasion has been sublime, dull or plain awful. For a dinner party given by friends, a telephone call thanking them will suffice and the same applies for a drinks or casual evening party, but for a slightly more formal dinner and for house guests a letter is still in order.

✱   At one time, it was 'not done' in thank-you letters to make what might be thought of as personal comments such as remarking on the food (especially if it might have been indifferently prepared by a resident cook), or on people's houses and their decor. These restrictions have now been abandoned which makes the letter-writer's task a great deal easier.

✱   Letters should be written as soon as possible, but certainly no later than a week after you have been entertained. Ladies can use Correspondence Cards to thank friends for dinner parties, but if it is the first time you have been a guest in someone's house, a proper letter would be preferable.

'Manners are the happy ways of doing things. If they are superficial so are the dewdrops which give such a depth to the morning meadows.'

Conduct of Life, R W Emerson (1803–82)

---

*U*se of the Telephone

✱   Few hosts object to guests making the occasional local telephone call, but it is courteous to ask permission from a member of the household before picking up the receiver. In some countries, local telephone calls are either free or charged at a flat rate, but in others are charged on a time basis, in which case be as brief as possible or offer to pay for the call.

✱   If making a long distance or international call, you should certainly offer to pay for it.

Paul Getty became so incensed by his guests running up astronomical bills, he installed pay-phones in all his homes while another gentle-man of similar wealth hid his telephones in cupboards. Clearly, it is difficult to hand a millionaire cash for a call and it can be equally as embarrassing with those in more straightened circumstances, whose need is greater, but cash can be left discreetly, in an envelope or a small present given.

* Inevitably, it is sometimes necessary for both business and personal reasons to give someone your host's number, but it should not be handed out casually to all and sundry who might like to call for a chat. Few things are more irritating than being unable to use your own telephone because a guest is permanently en-gaged on it, even if they are receiving, rather than making the call. It is polite, if you have left the number somewhere to say so on arrival. When giving another's number, state, as accu-rately as possible, at what time and for how long you will be there so that they are not bothered by calls for you after your departure or way in advance of your arrival.

> 'It is not learning, it is not virtue about which people inquire in society. It's manners.'
>
> Sketches in London, Thackeray (1811–63)

The Polite Child

The Victorian premise that children should be 'seen and not heard' was unnecessarily (and unnaturally) harsh and some relaxing of these draconian rules was clearly essential for the happiness of both children and their parents. However, children do need some form of discipline as there are few things more unappealing than an ill-mannered child.

In her book of *Etiquette* published in 1922, Emily Post summed it up neatly when she wrote: 'No young human being, any more than a dog, has the least claim to attractiveness unless it is trained to manners and obedience. The child that whines, interrupts, fusses, fidgets and does nothing that it is told to do, has not the least power of attraction for any one, even though it may have the features of an angel and be dressed like a picture. Another that may have no claim to beauty whatever, but that is sweet and nicely behaved exerts charm over everyone.'

Children are the greatest mimics in the world and will always ape their elders: so example is the best and most successful way of teaching children the rudiments of manners. To no one could this have been more brutally and sadly brought home than the fourth Earl of Chesterfield (1694–1773). From the time his

Illegitimate son, Philip Stanhope, was seven until his untimely death at the age of 36, Lord Chesterfield bombarded him with letters on the subject of manners and behaviour. For example, he would admonish him to: 'Know then, that as learning, honour and virtue are absolutely necessary to gain you the esteem and admiration of mankind, politeness and good-breeding are equally necessary to make you welcome and agreeable in conversation and common life. Great talents as honour, virtue, learning and parts are above the generality of the world ... but all people are judges of the lesser talents, such as civility, affability and an obliging, agreeable address and manner.'

Despite all this advice, Philip Stanhope grew into a shy, diffident, gauche man whom Boswell described as 'kind but clumsy and sloppy'— just the sort of person his poor father abhorred! On the death of his son, Lord Chesterfield turned his attentions on his godson and distant cousin who was to inherit the title, writing him 236 letters in a similar vein. Unfortunately, it proved again that the mere stroke of the pen, no matter how earnestly applied, is insufficient without the example, for Madame D'Arblay noted in her diary that the fifth earl had 'as little good breeding as any man I ever met with'.

$\mathscr{P}$s and Qs

 'Minding one's Ps and Qs' was one of the British Nanny's favourite expressions, referring to 'Pleases and Thank yous', still one of the simplest but most important expressions of good manners. It costs nothing to say, even if

A trick that everyone abhors
In Little Girls is slamming Doors.
A Wealthy Banker's Little Daughter
Who Lived in Palace Green, Bayswater
(by name Rebecca Offendort)
Was given to this Furious Sport.

She would deliberately go
And Slam the door like Billy-ho!
To make her Uncle Jacob start.
She was not really bad at heart,
But only rather rude and wild:
She was an aggravating child ...

  Cautionary Tales, Hilaire Belloc (1907)

someone is being paid for a service and might be considered to be a social inferior. People with the best breeding and the best manners are always polite to everyone, no matter what they perceive the other's social standing to be.

* Under the banner of Nanny's Ps and Qs came a host of other points. Some trifling, like eating bread and butter before cake at tea, but others form the basis of manners throughout society, such as not losing one's temper in public, not interrupting another when they are speaking, not bragging about new clothes, toys and other possessions to others who are less fortunate, and similar selfish behaviour.

* Above all, the British Nanny, who was frequently older than her charges' mother, taught children respect for their elders. They automatically stood up when an older person came into the room. They never publicly defied them and learned to listen attentively to their grandfather or other elderly relative, even if they were repeating a story for the third time— surely a valuable lesson for later life!

> 'He pointed—a vulgarism a good tutor would have corrected.'
>
> The Crime Wave at Blandings,
> P G Wodehouse (1881–1975)

*A*ddressing People

* It was not until the nineteenth century that children dared to address their parents as 'Mama' and 'Papa' or ' Mother' and 'Father'. Prior to that, they called them 'Madam' and 'Sir' or 'My Lady' and 'My Lord'. In the eighteenth century, the use of christian names was very limited with siblings referring to each other as 'brother' and 'sister' rather than by name.

At the close of the twentieth century, Christian names are used more freely than ever before, but children should still address an adult as Mr, Miss or Mrs until such time as the older person asks them to call him (or her) by his Christian name.

*P*resents

* Few things provide a present-giver with more pleasure than a letter of thanks, no matter how brief. A letter from a five-year-old simply saying 'Dear Aunt Emma, Thank you for my lovely doll', with perhaps a little drawing, is infinitely preferable to most people than a long, effusive letter from the child's mother.

* If a small gift is presented in person for a birthday or similar occasion and the donor has been thanked at the time, a letter is unnecessary. However, if it is an expensive present, even if the giver has been thanked, a letter is generally appreciated. If the present has not been delivered personally, a letter is essential. Quite apart from being rude and ungrateful, the donor has no way of knowing if the present has ever been received.

* Sadly, many adults do not put this practice into reverse and write and thank the child for a present they have received. It may have been the parent who actually paid for the present, but often the child has helped choose it and a letter thanking him or her will not only thrill the child but set a good example as well.

> *'Shoddy table manners have broken up many a happy bond.'*
>
> Colette-Gigi (1945)

'THE STORY OF FIDGETY PHILIP'

'Let me see if Philip can
Be a little gentleman;
Let me see if he is able
To sit still for once at table':
Thus Papa bade Phil behave;
And Mamma looked very grave.
But fidgety Phil,
He won't sit still . . .

See the naughty, restless child
Growing still more rude and wild,
Till his chair falls over quite.
Philip screams with all his might,
Catches at the cloth, but then
That makes matters worse again.
Down upon the ground they fall,
Glasses, plates, knives forks and all . . .

Where is Philip, where is he?
Fairly covered up you see!
Cloth and all are lying on him.
What a terrible to-do!
Dishes, glasses, snapt in two!
Here a knife and there a fork!
Philip, this is cruel work.

Struwwelpeter, Dr Heinrich Hoffman (1903)

'To mistake or forget names; to speak of Mr
What-d'ye-call-him, or Mrs Thingum or
How-d'ye- call hers, is excessively awkward
and ordinary.'

Lord Chesterfield (1741)

Table Manners

Table manners need to be instilled into a child as early as possible for they are not something that comes to *any* toddler naturally. Poor table manners are unattractive enough in a child but can be quite offensive in an adult. Lord Chesterfield's uncouth man who 'eats with his knife to the great danger of his mouth, picks his teeth with his fork and puts his spoon, which has been in his throat twenty times, into the dishes again . . . (and) generally daubes himself with soup and grease' is hardly a pleasant dining companion.

✳ Convention has it that children should sit up straight and not fidget and wave their arms about; use their cutlery neatly and quietly so that they do not make a scraping noise on the plate and place their knife (or spoon) and fork together when they have finished eating; eat quietly, not put too much food in their mouth at once and not speak with their mouth full; wipe their fingers on table napkins—not the mat or tablecloth in front of them—and generally behave in a socially acceptable manner.

✳ When eating in a restaurant or at a formal meal in someone else's house, considerate children wait until they are told to be seated—not just automatically sit themselves down, particularly when there is an elderly person present.

✳ Bread is traditionally broken before it is buttered and is not cut with a knife. The origin of this custom can be traced back to The Last Supper when Christ *broke* the bread, and cutting bread is considered unlucky by some people.

Cutlery

Using a different knife and fork for each course of a meal is a custom which has only developed over the last century and remains peculiarly Anglo Saxon. On the Continent, even at grand dinner parties, the same knife and fork is still used for all the courses (other than the soup and dessert for which spoons are essential). Everyone is provided with rests to place the cutlery on when the plates are removed, to prevent their soiling the tablecloth. This practice is also carried out by the British Royal Family when they dine at home alone.

In terms of European history, cutlery sets are a comparatively recent phenomenon. The Romans, as well as the early Britons, used spoons made of wood, horn, pewter or silver for eating soups, stews and other liquid food which could not be eaten with the fingers.

'If any competent person should institute a knife, fork and spoon drill and should offer to give private lessons in the use of these formidable weapons he might easily make a fortune. The knife is the easiest of the dread trio to manage, if you can successfully resist the temptations to thrust it into the mouth, which beset so many people.'

Florence Howe Hall (1887)

Knives were essential for cutting meat at the table and in medieval England, when food was eaten off trenchers of bread rather than plates, and put into the mouth with fingers, people took their own knives into meals. These were sturdy affairs, with pointed tips, but in France in 1669 Cardinal Richelieu's sensibilities were so offended by the sight of one diner picking his teeth with his knife he decreed that, in future, all dinner knives must have rounded blades. Ever keen to emulate Continental manners, fashionable society in Britain quickly adopted these more modern knives and the classic rounded, genteel, steel table knife was born.

Forks did not appear in general use for another century. Prior to that it was 'not customary for a host to supply his guests with forks who, if fastidious enough to require them, were expected to bring them in their pockets.' Indeed, the practice of giving an infant a knife, fork and spoon or 'nef' as a christening present can be traced back to the days when young children of noble birth, sent as pages to the homes of other noblemen, were expected to take their own 'nef' with them. By the start of the nineteenth century, most wealthy households had cutlery sets, not only for themselves but also for their guests although travelling sets of cutlery were still quite common.

Fish knives and forks were a Victorian invention. Prior to that, fish was eaten with a steel knife in the same way as meat, but it was remarked that the steel tainted the delicate flavour of the fish, giving it a slightly metallic taste. It then became fashionable to use a silver

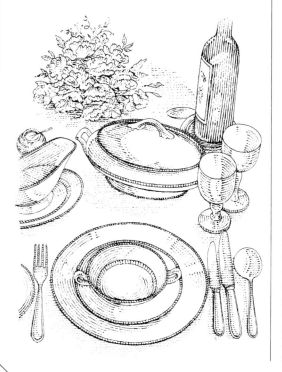

fork in the left hand and a crust of bread in the right to push the fish on to the fork, until one day a noted *bon viveur* hit upon the idea of using two silver forks. This novel method became quite the vogue until an astute cutlery manufacturer realized that the simple answer to eating fish delicately—an overriding Victorian obsession—was to produce a silver 'knife' for fish.

Soup spoons appeared on the scene even later. In *Manners and Rules of Good Society*, readers are advised to eat their soup with a tablespoon. This was preferable to a dessertspoon as ladies, in particular, were not expected to take more than half a ladleful of soup and the use of a larger spoon ensured that it was eaten while still hot. Dessertspoons do not generally seem to find favour with the writer at all, only being recommended for very liquid desserts; a fork is suggested even for jellies. Dessert knives and forks were used extensively for eating fruit and she goes into considerable detail as to how to eat every kind of fruit from grapes, apples, nectarines and figs to pineapples.

Today there are very few hard and fast rules about how tables are laid, how food is presented or how it is eaten. But there is one golden rule. Never feel embarrassed if, by chance, you have used the wrong utensil. It is a mistake which has been made by millionaires, peers of the realm, and bishops. Using a large, rather than a small, knife for your bread, for example, is no problem anyway but do not try to cover up you error if you find yourself trying to cut a steak with a fish knife! Simply smile at your host or hostess, apologize for your mistake and ask for a replacement.

The Good Sport

'It is not whether you win or lose, but how you play the game' has always been the maxim for playing sport in Britain. An attitude, it has to be said, that has not always met with the approval of every member of society—more than a few would have a passing sympathy with the character in A G Macdonald's *England Their England* who, on hearing that his country had been annihilated by the Australians in a Test Match, expostulated, 'It all comes of treating it as a game. We don't take things seriously enough in this country, sir, damnation take it all' and stomped off.

Generally, though, the manner in which a game is played has always been considered to be of greater importance than whether you end up the conqueror or the vanquished. While this rather relaxed stance has finally been eroded in the highest echelons of competitive sport, to be replaced by a more professional approach, it still remains the first essential at the lower levels. This does not mean that people do not try to win, just that they do not (and, according to an unwritten law, should not) appear outwardly aggressive and determined and also should submit to the final outcome of any match with good grace, congratulating or commiserating with their opponent and thanking the referee or umpire.

Most sports carry with them a considerable degree of frustration, which is often partly their attraction. One day you might play well, shoot well or catch several fish, and the following day is an unmitigated disaster on all fronts. However angry you may be with yourself, the good sport does not lose his temper or start swearing— even if the invectives are aimed at himself! He may admit after the match or at the end of the day that he was cross with himself, but *never* during play.

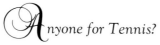

Anyone for Tennis?

Real tennis, a game played with racquets and balls made of tightly compressed rags with a woollen cover, on the stone floor of a courtyard or an enclosed tennis court, was popular in Tudor England. Henry VIII was the champion of England, hardly surprising as no one dared oppose him and he was always allowed to win!

> '*To be a good sportsman, one must be a stoic and never show rancor in defeat, or triumph in victory, or irritation, no matter what annoyance is encountered. One who can not help sulking, or explaining, or protesting when the loser, or exulting when the winner, has no right to take part in games or contests.*'
>
> *Etiquette,* Emily Post (1922)

The magnificent court he played on can still be viewed at Hampton Court.

With the development of the bouncing rubber ball, lawn tennis became fashionable as a country house game in the 1870s. At a time when big house parties took place throughout the summer and guests had to be entertained, it quickly found favour, for it was a sport that both sexes could participate in. As they played with many more than four people on the court at once, it also occupied a good proportion of the guests. It was not entirely a summer sport either, for an engraving appeared in *Punch* in 1876 of lawn tennis being played on ice—for which they presumably reverted to using the old real tennis ball.

Professional tennis today bears little resemblance to the elegant games played on the lawns of England in the late nineteenth century, but the spirit in which the game is played remains all-important. Sadly, there has been an increasing amount of professional gamesmanship over the past few years, but it is to be hoped that this never filters through to the lower levels of the game. Children are particularly vulnerable to its influence for they ape the behaviour of their heroes and heroines, and parents, or those in charge of them, should stamp out any signs of such behaviour before it is allowed to develop—it has no place in good sportsmanship and so needs to be discouraged.

✱   The etiquette of tennis is purely a quesion of good manners and consideration of others, and this is especially true when playing doubles. Obviously, if you make an appallingly bad unforced error, you should apologize to your

partner, but there is no need to apologize every time you lose a point, for that can become irritating. Equally, when your partner plays a very good shot, you should congratulate him (or her)—everybody enjoys praise.

✱ There are several other standard points of etiquette to be followed when playing tennis: congratulate your opponent on any exceptional shot he makes or, if he plays a shot you are unable to reach, you should nod your head or lift your hand to acknowledge that the shot beat you. Don't hit the ball in your partner's half of the court, unless by prior arrangement, or if your partner has been unable to reach the ball and has called 'yours'.

✱ When there is no umpire present, it is not always possible to tell if a ball is in or out but you must be quite fair and if there is any disagreement and your opponent(s) is (are) not happy, offer to replay the point.

DRESS

No matter what level the game is played at, 'whites' are the order of the day: white shirts, shorts and jumpers for the men, and white shirts, shorts or skirts or white dresses and jumpers for the ladies, as well as white socks and shoes for both. When warming up, track suits can be worn in cold weather and these can be of any colour.

olf

The game of golf is an ancient Scottish tradition. At St Andrews, universally known as the 'home of golf', the game has been played since the fifteenth century. In 1754, '22 noblemen and gentlemen being admirers of the ancient and healthful exercise of the golf' founded a club, which received royal patronage from King William in 1834.

Women in Scotland have played golf for centuries. Mary Queen of Scots was a great enthusiast and has the distinction of being the only known lady golfer to be beheaded—a fate which many gentlemen feel should have befallen a few more! When it was mooted in 1893 that there should be a ladies' competition, the British male champion decried the idea, claiming that 'Women will fall out and quarrel as they always do...Physically and temperamentally they are unsuited to the game.' Everyone makes mistakes!

Golf is an unusual sport, for although you have an opponent, your game is actually pitted against the vagaries of the course and is quite independent of the quality of his (or her) game. Consequently, opponents are most frequently referred to as partners. The fierce kind of rivalry that exists between opponents on the tennis court is rare and the system of handicapping means that two people of widely varying abilities can have an enjoyable game together.

* In addition to the rules of the game, there are a few unwritten laws that should be observed if you do not wish to have difficulty in finding partners. You never offer unsolicited advice to your partner, even if he (or she) is playing badly, nor ask which club he has used for a shot or suggest one. If he loses his ball, you should assist him in trying to find it.

* When he is taking his shot, you should stand at 90 degrees to him. You must remain very still and silent and that includes coughing, blowing your nose or doing anything else which might cause him to lose his concentration, such as making a sudden movement. Above all, to be an enjoyable partner, no matter how pleased you may be with your own game on any one day, you should not mention it and, if your partner's is not up to scratch, you should commiserate with him. Tomorrow the tables may be turned.

DRESS

Fashions in golfing attire change not only from decade to decade but also from year to year. Today, few people would be seen dead on a golf course wearing the loud checked plus-two suits beloved of Wodehouse's Bertie Wooster! If invited to play as a guest at a friend's club, it is perhaps wise to err on the conservative, rather than the garish, side and remember never to walk into a clubhouse wearing spiked golfing shoes.

KEEPING YOUR DISTANCE

Not driving off the tee until the people in front are out of range is not only good manners but prudence—unless you wish to be accused of causing Grevious Bodily Harm. Should one accidentally drive too soon, the culprit should yell 'fore' quickly, to warn those ahead of the approaching ball. One old lady of 97 attributed her longevity to spreadeagling herself every time she heard the word!

P G Wodehouse's golfing character The Oldest Member is also liberal with his advice on the subject.

'Driving into people is a thing one always regrets. I have driven into people in my golfing days and I was always sorry later. There is something about the reproachful eye of the victim as you meet it subsequently in the bar of the clubhouse which cannot fail to jar a man of sensibility. Like a wounded oyster. Wait till they are out of distance says the good book.'

The Team Spirit

* When playing any team game, be it football, rugby, cricket, hockey, lacrosse or polo, everyone must remember that they are part of a team and not try to seek personal glory. A side composed of people each playing an individual game is not only likely to be defeated but will provide poor entertainment for any spectators.

* At a social level, especially, it is only too easy for a 'too many chiefs and not enough Indians' situation to arise and it is important that all team members obey the captain. Very often, one or two members of a side possess superior skills but they should not attempt to shoot all the goals or take all the wickets. Every member of a side is important, no matter how small their contribution—a cricket eleven with only ten men or a rugby fifteen with only fourteen suffer a severe handicap. If one member of the team is not playing well, he (or she) should be given encouragement by his team-mates, for he is doubtless even more aware of the fact than they are, and needs a little boost to ease his mortification.

❋ Above all, it must never be forgotten that not only is the referee's or umpire's decision final, but his judgement should not be questioned. Few things show lack of sportsmanship more than arguments with the referee. No matter how wrong the decision may appear to be to the player or how harsh the judgement, a true sportsman accepts it stoically.

❋ 'I told this story once to the late Jack Fingleton who, in his latter days, was a disappointed observer of the decline of attitudes, both on and off the cricket field. I think what finally polished Jack off was the news that the England team to visit Australia contained a cricketer wearing an earring. Aluminium bats, purple sweaters, white balls and black sightscreens had already weakened Jack's will to live, but a cricketer wearing jewellery finally persuaded him to give up altogether.

Anyhow, after telling Jack about my run-in with the quick bowler, he reminded me that psychological warfare had always been a part of cricket, but what had changed over the years was the manner of delivery. The silken, humorous insult had been replaced with vulgar abuse. The Australians, who have a way with words, called it "sledging".

As an example of how it used to be, Jack told the story of making his debut for his club in Sydney and walking to the wicket with C G Macartney, the legendary Australian test cricketer. The young Fingleton trotted alongside the master as he strode to the wicket, eager to get everything right, to impress on his debut. Their walk to the middle was made in silence until, as they approached the wicket, Macartney said to his partner, "Remember, young man, watch out for the first ball."

Jack wondered what the message might mean and decided that Macartney was telling him to be on his toes for the quick single. As Macartney settled down to face the first ball, the young Fingleton was trembling with eagerness and excitement. The fast bowler thundered in and as he approached the wicket so Macartney began a leisurely stroll down the wicket towards him. Jack was also backing up so the overall picture must have been of three people moving towards each other on a narrow pavement.

As the bowler bowled, Macartney continuing his stroll, straight drove the ball back at head height causing Jack, the bowler and the umpire to fling themselves to the ground. The ball hit the sightscreen with a terrible crack and rebounded fifty yards onto the field.

Jack said that as he, the umpire and the bowler untangled themselves from the heap he was aware of Macartney standing next to him leaning nonchalantly on his bat. "See what I mean about that first ball, young Fingleton? Always hit it back smack between their eyes. They don't much like it," he said smiling disarmingly at the bowler.'

Punch, Michael Parkinson (1984)

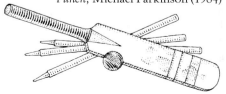

unting

For anyone with the necessary skills in horsemanship, few things are more thrilling than a day's hunting and many hunts are very happy to accept visitors for the day. If in any doubt as to whether or not visitors are accepted by a hunt, check with the Hunt Secretary for in order to hunt with some packs you have to be invited by a member. There are a number of strict rules of etiquette in the hunting field which everyone, including visitors, is expected to know and adhere to.

* On arrival at the meet, always say 'Good Morning Master' to the Master (even if you sat next to him at dinner the night before and called him by his Christian name). The treasurer or secretary will be on the lookout for any new faces and will come and ask for your cap for the day, but if he misses you, you must make sure that you find him at some stage of the day. At the meet, endeavour to discover who the Field Master is as he is the person you must follow.

* Hounds cost a good deal of money to rear and are precious to the hunt so, on no account, must you either 'ride over' them on narrow tracks or allow your mount to kick a hound. If hounds are coming down a road, your horse's head must face into the road to avoid any chance of this. Everyone hunting (including the members) is a guest of the Master and he (or she) is at liberty to send home anyone he feels is behaving badly.

* It is not the done thing to cut into anyone at a jump, nor to take a jump until the person in front is safely over. The last person through a gate always shuts it, however difficult it is, and the person immediately before the gate shutter should wait until the task has been completed. Followers always keep to the edges of fields and other cultivated land, and take care of farmers' livestock. If damage is caused, an offer to pay for it is made.

* At the end of the day, followers always thank the Master or Field Master and say 'Good night' even if it is only afternoon.

One of the most flamboyant post-war figures was Nubar Gulbenkian who, among other things, drove around London in a taxi with a Rolls Royce engine and a gold basketwork body because the vehicle could 'turn on a sixpence—whatever that is'. An habitué of The Ritz, at one time he had a permanent suite there and his devotion to The Ritz kitchen can be witnessed by his comment that 'The best number for a dinner party is two—myself and a dam' good head waiter.'

On his debut in the hunting field with the Pytchley, when a guest of the Spencers at Althorp, Gulbenkian astounded many of the venerable members of this ancient pack by turning out on his own Arab steed in immaculate hunting attire—but with a large and exotic orchid in his buttonhole.

DRESS

Both gentlemen and ladies wear breeches, black hunting coats or jackets, white shirts, stocks held in place with a stock pin, and black boots when out hunting. Ladies can also wear blue jackets and both sexes can wear waistcoats. For a day's cub hunting, black jackets are never worn, but a tweed, or similar, hacking jacket is. At one time, gentlemen wore silk top hats and ladies bowlers but an increasing awareness of safety has resulted in most members of the field now wearing black caps or crash helmets with a black velvet cover. At one time it was thought very bad form if the cap had any form of chinstrap but these days the efficacy of the headcovering is of greater importance than its appearance. All ladies should wear nets to keep their hair in place.

HUNTING AND SHOOTING TERMS

Hunting and shooting are sports with their own private language and it is advisable to be versed in the principal terms if planning a day's sport.

Hunting

Brace   meaning two, and the number by which foxes are counted. Half a brace equals one fox, one and a half brace equals three foxes.

Brush   the tail of the fox.

Cap   the fee required for a day's hunting.

Couple   meaning two, and the number by which hounds are counted. Half a couple equals one hound, three and a half couple equals 7 hounds.

Covert   (pronounced 'cover')—the area of woodland, kale, scrub, etc in which a fox is hoped to be found.

Earth   the underground burrow of a fox.

Field   the mounted followers of the hunt.

Gone to ground   the fox has returned to an earth.

Hounds   always referred to as 'hounds' and not 'the hounds'.

Hunt servants   the paid employees of the hunt such as the kennel huntsman and whippers-in.

Line   the direction taken by the fox.

Mask   the head of the fox.

Pack   the collective name for hounds. There are bitch packs and dog packs.

Meet   the location where the hunt starts. A *lawn meet* indicates that the meeting place is outside somebody's house and that food and drinks are likely to be served.

Shooting

Bag   the number of game killed in the day.

Beaters   the men (and sometimes women and older children) who drive the birds out of the covert towards the guns.

> '*To prove that he knew how to have been a gentleman with a great estate, he shows that he can behave like a gentleman without an estate.*'
>
> Compleat English Gentleman,
> Daniel Defoe (1729)

Shooting is not a dangerous sport in the same way that hunting or skiing are but it must never be forgotten that guns are lethal weapons which kill and most of the etiquette surrounding shooting is centred on safety.

* Sportsmen always keep a gun unloaded when not shooting and to prove this, keep it broken. When talking to someone a gun is kept unloaded, as it is when the gun is put down, or when climbing over a gate or fence. A gun is never pointed at anyone and nobody leaves their butt or peg until instructed to, either by the host or his keeper, or until a signal is given at the end of a drive.

* Late attendance at a shoot is considered most impolite. On arrival, check with your host the rules regarding what can be shot, not only in the way of birds but also ground game such as hares, and vermin including squirrels and jays and, more especially, foxes. Different shoots have varying rules.

Brace meaning two, and the number by which birds are counted although these days pheasants are frequently counted by numbers.

Butt the position of each gun on a grouse moor, which usually takes the form of a small camouflaged area made of stone or turf. Butts are numbered so that each member of the party knows where to stand.

Covert as hunting, but the area where game is found.

Covey a group of grouse or partridges.

Drive each sweep of birds put up by the beaters.

Gun not only the implement used for shooting but a person using it.

Peg the position in the firing line of each gun when shooting birds other than grouse.

Runner a wounded bird which is unable to fly.

> *'What I admire in the order to which you belong is that they do live in the air: that they excel in athletic sports: that they can only speak one language: and that they never read. This is not a complete education, but it is the highest education since the Greek.'*
>
> *English Gentlemen,*
> Benjamin Disraeli (1804–1881)

* The only kind of dog welcomed at a shoot is a properly trained gun dog.

* Taking an insufficient amount of cartridges implies that you did not think there was likely to be very good sport. Equally, keeping some of your supply discreetly out of sight, in case the day does not live up to expectations, is considerate.

* Do not chatter while waiting for the game as the human voice frightens birds and you can ruin the day for everybody.

* Do not poach your neighbour's bird—it is not only bad manners but can be dangerous.

DRESS

There is no specific dress code for shooting but most gentlemen prefer to wear some form of knickerbockers (either plus-twos or -fours which can be worn with long socks or stockings and boots) and a jacket appropriate to the weather (either tweed or waxed). At some shoots, a tie is obligatory, whereas at others polo-necked shirts are quite in order.

What is far more important than the actual clothes, not only for guns, but for any companions who may be with them, is the colour worn. These should be muted greens, browns

> *'If a man is a gentleman, he knows quite enough, and if he is not a gentleman, whatever he knows is bad for him.'*
>
> Oscar Wilde (1854–1900)

and purples so that they blend into the background and do not frighten the game. The only other essential piece of equipment for guns is hats—unless one is possessed of a remarkable head of hair with no traces of grey!

Fishing

All the comments made in the next few paragraphs refer to game fishing, as distinct from coarse fishing which is a separate sport. Unlike many other sports, fishing is a solitary hobby. That does not mean that you cannot be on the same boat or river bank as friends but fish are very sensitive to noise so one cannot spend time in idle gossip.

* Fishermen (or women) always allow plenty of space between themselves and others, so that other people and their water aren't disturbed. It is generally accepted that there should be only one rod in any recognized pool at any one time, from either bank.

* If one fisherman is spinning and the other fly fishing, the spinner gives way to fly for he (or she) can fish the water after the fly fisherman has departed, but it is not possible the other way round.

DRESS

Bright colours are avoided for they alarm the fish and make them aware of the fisherman's presence. Hats are always worn as a matter of safety in case of a miscast. It is wise not to walk into a river unless wearing waders, for depths can vary suddenly and, in one stride, the water an go from just over the ankles to over the top of wellington boots. If planning to venture out into the middle of a river, wearing chest waders, carry a wading stick so that the terrain in front can be prodded to discover if there are any sudden shelves which might prove dangerous. Some form of sunglasses are also recommended to protect the eyes from glare off the water. These may also prove advantageous in allowing one to see into the water.

Gaming

Gambling is as old as Man himself and takes a variety of different forms but, over the centuries, rules of behaviour have evolved which a wise person does not break.

*   Never gamble more that you can afford to lose. Gambling debts may not be recoverable by law but bookmakers, casino owners and the like have long memories and will never let you forget—or escape. Owing your bookmaker may cause sleepless nights but in society that is not nearly as serious a crime as owing money to a friend (or even a foe) to whom you have lost at cards. That is dishonourable behaviour which cannot be condoned under any circumstances.

*   Where games of cards are concerned, always check the rules before joining a school. You may think you know the rules of a certain game backwards but different sets of people have different variations, so double check.

*   When playing cards, it is wise not to show too much elation when winning nor too much disappointment when losing, however much the wallet may be hurting. Similarly at the races, keep a check over any frustration you may feel at losing but you can display your pleasure at winning—especially if you buy the champagne!

Index